METALS

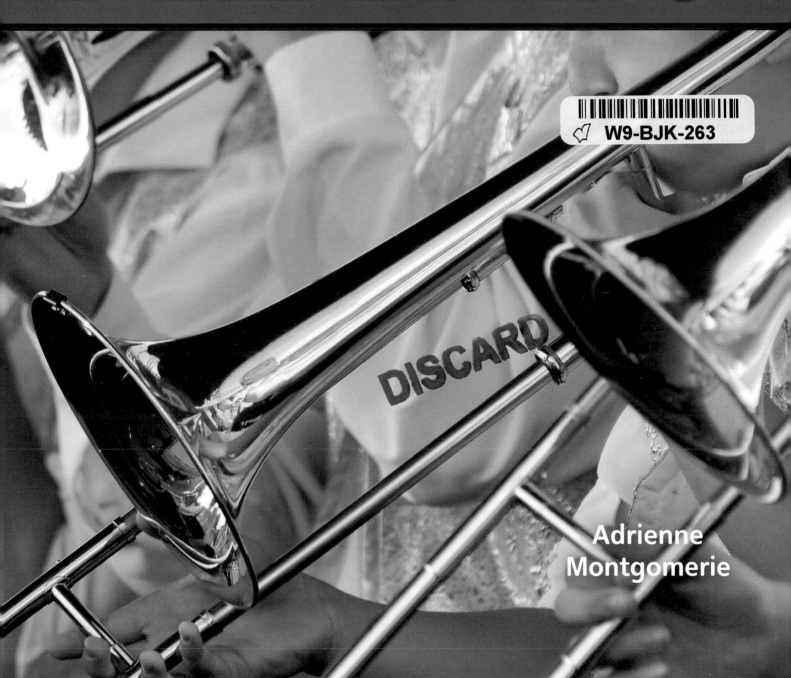

W9-BJK-263

DISCARD

Adrienne
Montgomerie

Crabtree Publishing Company

www.crabtreebooks.com

Crabtree Publishing Company

www.crabtreebooks.com

Author: Adrienne Montogomerie
Publishing plan research and development:
  Sean Charlebois, Reagan Miller
  Crabtree Publishing Company
Project Editor: Tom Jackson
Editor: Adrianna Morganelli
Proofreader: Crystal Sikkens
Project Coordinator: Kathy Middleton
Designer: Karen Perry
Cover Design: Demetra Peppas
Picture Researcher: Sophie Mortimer
Managing Editor: Tim Harris
Art Director: Jeni Child
Editorial Director: Lindsey Lowe
Children's Publisher: Anne O'Daly
Production and Print Coordinator: Katherine Berti
Prepress Technician: Katherine Berti

Photographs:
Cover: iStockphoto
Interior: Library of Congress: 25t, **NASA:** 25b, **Science
Photo Library:** 11; **Shutterstock:** 6, 13, 16b, 19t, Imfoto
12, J.T. Baskin Photo 15t, Marcel Clemens 5b, 29t,
Jordache 22, Keith LeBlanc 29b, Jane McIlroy 16t,
Dimitry Melnik 4, Varina & Jay Patel 10, Paul Prescott
20, Sachek 28, SlipFloat 23b, Thorsten Schier 18;
Thinkstock: BananStock 27b, Hemera 23t, 26, Ingram
Publishing 15b, iStockphoto 5t, 8, 9, 21, 24, 27t, Lifesize
7, Photodisc 14, Photos.com 4, 5b, 6, 7, 8, 11t, 20, 29.

All artwork and diagrams © Brown Bear Books Ltd.

Produced for the Crabtree Publishing Company
by Brown Bear Books Ltd.

Library and Archives Canada Cataloguing in Publication

Montgomerie, Adrienne
    Metals / Adrienne Montgomerie.

(Why chemistry matters)
Includes index.
Issued also in electronic format.
ISBN 978-0-7787-4231-9 (bound).--ISBN 978-0-7787-4235-7 (pbk.)

    1. Metals--Juvenile literature. I. Title. II. Series: Why
chemistry matters

QD171.M66 2012   j546'.3   C2012-906391-6

Library of Congress Cataloging-in-Publication Data

CIP available at Library of Congress

Crabtree Publishing Company

www.crabtreebooks.com 1-800-387-7650

Printed in the U.S.A./112012/FA20121012

Copyright © **2013 CRABTREE PUBLISHING COMPANY.** All rights reserved. No part of this publication may be
reproduced, stored in a retrieval system or be transmitted in any form or by any means, electronic, mechanical, recording
photocopying, or otherwise, without the prior written permission of Crabtree Publishing Company. In Canada: We
acknowledge the financial support of the Government of Canada through the Canada Book Fund for our publishing activities.

**Published in
Canada
Crabtree Publishing**
616 Welland Ave.
St. Catharines, ON
L2M 5V6

**Published in the
United States
Crabtree Publishing**
PMB 59051
350 Fifth Avenue, 59th Floor
New York, New York 10118

**Published in the
United Kingdom
Crabtree Publishing**
Maritime House
Basin Road North, Hove
BN41 1WR

**Published in
Australia
Crabtree Publishing**
3 Charles Street
Coburg North
VIC, 3058

Contents

NOV 2013
R0440204119

What Is a Metal?

Most **elements** are **metals**. They are hard and shiny substances that carry electricity and heat well.

Elements are the building blocks of the universe. There are 92 elements in nature, and they come together in different combinations to make all the substances around us. These natural substances, such as wood or water, can be simplified into their element ingredients. Elements are the simplest type of substance—they cannot be divided into any other ingredients. Every element is either a metal, a **non-metal**, or a **metalloid**. There are a total of 118 elements known today. The extra ones are not natural and have to be made in laboratories. About 95 elements are metals.

Metals are not all the same, but they do share a set of properties. Almost all are solid in normal conditions, and they are **lustrous**, which means their surfaces shine in the light.

Metals are dense solids. Only small amounts weigh a lot. That makes them ideal for use as weights.

Applying heat to metals causes them to become soft and flexible enough to bend into shapes. Very high temperatures, however, can cause most metals to melt.

Mercury

Only one metal is a liquid in normal conditions. This is mercury, sometimes known as quicksilver. Mercury was used in early thermometers because any rise in temperature makes the metal expand. The expanding liquid flows up the thermometer, showing the increase. (Cooler temperatures make the metal contract.) We now know that mercury is poisonous and so it is rarely used today. It can damage the brain and only a small amount can kill a person. In the 19th century, mercury was used to make felt hats. The metal poisoned many hatmakers making them go mad. A character known as the Mad Hatter appears in the book Alice in Wonderland.

Metals are also opaque, which means light cannot pass through them. (The opposite of opaque is transparent. Window glass is transparent.) Metals are also flexible and can be bent and twisted without breaking. Scientists describe them as **malleable**—they can be hammered into flat sheets—and **ductile**—they can be pulled into thin wires.

Metal wires are used to carry electric currents. Heat also flows through them easily. All these metallic properties can be explained by understanding the **atoms** that make up metals.

Inside Metals

Everything is made of tiny particles called atoms. These are the smallest possible units of an element. The atomic structure of metallic elements is what gives them their properties.

A pure sample of an element is made of just one type of atom. An atom is made of **electrons** circling a central nucleus of **protons** (and generally **neutrons**, too). Every element has a specific combination of particles in its atoms. That is what makes elements different from each other.

The electrons have a negative **charge**, while the protons have a positive charge. Their opposite charges attract each other, holding the atom together. The electrons are located in layers or shells that surround the nucleus. Each shell can hold a certain number of electrons. When one shell is full, any more electrons take up position in the next shell, slightly farther out from the nucleus.

Metal mirrors reflect light without jumbling it up so you can still see the image.

The electrons in the outermost shell are the ones that give atoms—and elements—their properties.

The outer shell of most atoms can hold eight electrons in total. In chemical reactions, atoms try to get full outer shells to become more stable. They form bonds with other atoms to do this. (For example, hydrogen and oxygen atoms bond into **molecules** of water.)

Most metal atoms have either one or two outer electrons (a very few have more). Because of this, metals react in the same way: they give away their outer electrons. The next shell down, which is already full, becomes their stable outer one.

Polishing Metal

Rub an old metal spoon with polish to make it shiny again. The polish wears off any non-metal dirt on the surface, revealing the metal atoms beneath. Light hitting the metals is absorbed by the atoms and then given straight out again. This makes the metal shine.

Electron Shells

*All atoms have electrons arranged in layers or shells. Metal atoms have only a few electrons in their outer **electron shells**. A few metals have three or four outer electrons, but nearly all others have just one or two outer electrons. The low number of outer electrons makes metals behave in similar ways.*

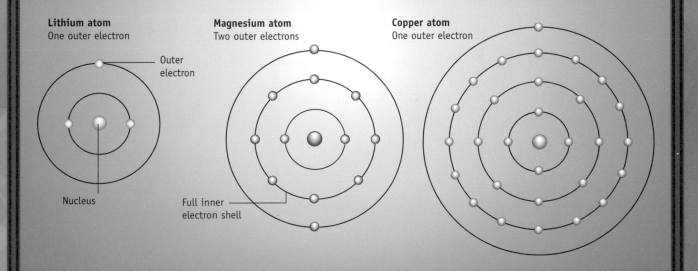

Lithium atom
One outer electron

Outer electron

Nucleus

Magnesium atom
Two outer electrons

Full inner electron shell

Copper atom
One outer electron

Conductors

Metals conduct heat and electricity very well. A "sea" of shared electrons inside carries the energy through the metal.

When a lot of metal atoms are close together, their outer electrons come loose. They form a "sea" of electrons that is shared equally by all the atoms. The pull between the electrons and the metal's atoms forms a "glue" that bonds them all together. This system is called a metallic bond. Metallic bonds are very strong, but the atoms can still move around inside without the bond breaking. That is what makes metals so flexible, ductile, and malleable. The bonds hold the metal together, but allow it to change in shape without breaking apart.

The shared electrons in metals are also free to move. Generally they vibrate back and forth but they can also flow in one direction through the metal. This feature is what makes metals excellent **conductors**. Conductors carry electric currents easily and also allow heat to spread through them. (The opposite of a conductor is an **insulator**.)

When an object is hot, the particles (atoms and free electrons) inside vibrate more powerfully. Imagine heating one end of a metal bar.

A toaster has metal wires inside that warm up when electricity runs through them. The hot wires cook the bread.

The free electrons rattle around inside the hot end and collide with slower ones farther along the metal, where it is cooler. These collisions pass energy through the metal's electron "sea." This is how heat gradually conducts from the hot end of the bar to the colder end.

An electric current is slightly different. The electrons are normally spread equally through the metal. However, if extra electrons are added to one part and taken away from another, the electrons begin to flow. They move from where there are too many electrons to where there are not enough. The flow of electrons carries energy with it, which makes electricity useful for powering machines. Non-metal insulators do not have any free electrons, so electric currents cannot form inside them.

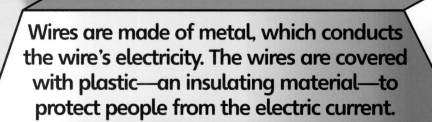

Wires are made of metal, which conducts the wire's electricity. The wires are covered with plastic—an insulating material—to protect people from the electric current.

Alkali Metals

The alkali metals is a group of reactive metals that includes lithium, sodium, and potassium.

The alkali metals form what is known as Group 1 in the periodic table. All members of this group have atoms with just one electron in the outer shell. This makes them highly reactive. All the atom has to do to react is lose that single electron. Having lost the negative charge from one electron, the atom turns into an **ion** with a positive charge of 1+. Positive ions are attracted to a negative ion. Negative ions form from the atoms of non-metal elements, which collect extra electrons instead of giving them away.

Sodium and potassium are used in nerves and muscles, helping us feel, move, and stay balanced.

The periodic table is a way of organizing the elements.

Periodic Table of Elements

Key:
- Non-metals
- Poor metals
- Metalloids
- Halogens
- Noble gases
- Transition metals
- Alkali metals
- Alkaline earth metals

The oppositely charged ions bond together to make molecules. Sodium, the most common alkali metal, reacts with the non-metal chlorine in this way. They form sodium chloride, the chemical name for common salt. This substance makes seawater taste salty and is also used to season food.

Alkali metals are named for the way the metals react with water. They produce substances called alkalies. An alkali is the opposite of an acid. One of the many uses of alkalies is to cure indigestion. Antacid tablets contain safe potassium alkalies that react with the acid from the stomach that is causing the problem. Lithium is used in other medicines that help the brain work better.

Flame Test Colors

Scientists can identify metals by the color of the flames they create when burned. This is called a flame test. Each metal produces a flame in a different color. Burning copper makes a bright green flame; lithium makes a deep red flame; potassium burns with a lilac flame; and a sodium flame is intense yellow. These colors appear even when the metals are combined with other elements. Astronomers can see the same colors in the light from distant stars. That shows us which elements are out in space and what stars are made of. Powdered metals are also added to fireworks to create colorful explosions.

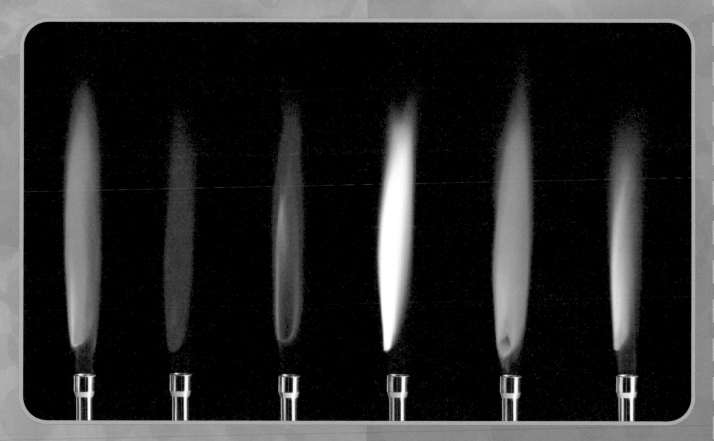

Alkaline Earth Metals

The alkaline earth metals form a second group of metallic elements. They include beryllium, magnesium, and calcium, and are often found in crystals and rocks.

Group 2 in the periodic table is known as the alkaline earth metals. The full list is beryllium, magnesium, calcium, strontium, barium, and radium. Like Group 1 metals, these elements also form alkalies when they react with water. However, the alkaline earth metals are less reactive than Group 1, and so are the alkalies they form.

Group 2 metals have atoms with two outer electrons and both must be given away during a reaction. Because these metals lose two electrons they form ions with a charge of 2+. (These positive charges come from the protons that remain in the atomic nucleus.) While one sodium ion (1+) bonds to one chloride ion (1−), to make sodium chloride, magnesium chloride is made from one magnesium ion (2+) and two chlorides.

Calcium is the most common alkaline earth metal. It is often found in calcium carbonate, a naturally occurring mineral that makes up limestone and other rocks. It is also used by snails, crabs, and shellfish to make tough shells.

Barium is a very heavy metal. It is used in hospitals to X-ray the stomach and intestines. A patient drinks a liquid mixed with barium powder. The powder fills the stomach so it shows up in X-ray images.

Emerald is a precious gem made mostly of beryl, a compound of beryllium.

Calcium Cascade

Limestone consists mostly of calcium carbonate, a compound containing a common alkaline earth metal. In Pamukkale, Turkey, the spring water has so much calcium carbonate mixed in with it that it creates cascades of limestone as the water trickles down the cliff.

Transition Metals

Most metals belong to a set called the transition metals. This group includes many of the most familiar metals, such as iron, copper, nickel, zinc, and even gold.

The world's coins are made from copper and nickel, which are mixed to produce different colors.

The transition metals form a large block of elements that sit in the middle of the periodic table. They form a transition, or "change," between Group 2 and the elements in Group 3 (some of which are metals).

The atoms of transition metals are arranged a little differently to those of other elements. Most have atoms with two electrons in their outer shell (a few have just one). This feature is what makes them metallic.

However, the transition metals also have empty spaces in the next electron shell down. The outer electrons are given away in some reactions, using the same process as Group 1 and Group 2 metals.

However, the transition metals can also receive electrons from other atoms, and they bond in unusual ways. The rusting process of iron, for example, involves this kind of reaction.

You may probably recognize many names of the transition metals, such as gold, silver, or mercury. Copper and iron are the most common. Copper is the best conductor of electricity and is used in all kinds of wiring. Iron is a very common metal—most of Earth's core, deep inside the planet, is made from it! Other transition metals are less well known. Tungsten has a very high **melting point** and so it is used in glowing electric heaters and light bulbs. Titanium is lightweight but strong and used for making aircraft.

Alloys

*An **alloy** is a mixture of metals. They are created by stirring two or more metals together when they are liquid. When cooled, the solid alloy has the characteristics of all its ingredients. Familiar alloys include bronze, which is a mixture of copper and tin, and brass, which is copper and zinc. Steel is an iron alloy with small amounts of carbon, which make it very strong. Stainless steel also contains chromium, which stops the iron from rusting. The Gateway Arch(above) in St. Louis, Missouri, is made from 142 12-foot (3.7 m) plates of stainless steel.*

Sunscreen contains zinc oxide, a white compound that includes a transition metal and that stops dangerous rays in sunlight from reaching the skin.

Corrosion

Pure metals corrode when they react with the oxygen, water, and other chemicals in the environment.

The most common form of **corrosion** is rust, which damages iron objects. Corrosion is a chemical reaction between the metal and oxygen in the air. Water is often involved in corrosion as well. The reaction turns the pure metal into a compound. The full chemical name for rust is iron oxide-hydroxide. The new material makes the metal weaker.

Copper objects, such as statues, turn green as they corrode; iron is covered in red-brown rust.

Protecting Metal from Corrosion

Method	Description	Example
Painting	Paint is spread on the surface	A car body
Oiling	Oil is spread on the surface	Iron frying pan
Electroplating	Electricity draws a corrosion-resistant metal onto the surface of another object	Chrome taps or wheel rims
Anodizing	A thin layer of corrosion on the surface shields the metal underneath	Aluminum computer case
Alloying	Corrosion-resistant metal added to protect the others	Stainless steel knife
Galvanizing	Layer of zinc reacts with corroding chemicals in place of the metal beneath	Ship, roofing, outdoor nails

Rust takes up more space than the iron it forms from. As it spreads the rust creates cracks in the metal.

The best way to stop corrosion is to protect the metal from the air or water. Something as simple as a coat of paint can stop rust, but even a tiny hole in it will let the corrosion in.

Rusting a Nail

Fill three glasses with water and put a nail in each. The first nail is galvanized. The second is a regular nail (scratching it with sandpaper will ensure it rusts). The third is also a regular nail but coat it in cooking oil first and pour a little more oil on top of the water. After a week, only the second nail will have rusted. The zinc layer protects the iron in the first one, while the oil prevents oxygen in the water from getting to the third nail.

Left to right: galvanized nail, iron nail, and oiled nail

Poor Metals

The poor set of metals has some unusual properties. For example, lead is very soft while aluminum is very lightweight.

The wires carrying electricity between pylons are made from lightweight aluminum.

A few metal elements have atoms with three or four electrons in their outer shells. One of them, barium, even has five. These metals are called poor metals because their metallic features are often very weak.

They are generally unreactive compared to other metals. Lead and tin are some of the few metals that are found pure in nature instead of being combined with other elements. They are also very soft metals and both melt at low temperatures. In addition, most of these metals are poor conductors of heat and electricity.

Nevertheless, the poor metals have their uses. Gallium and indium are used to make **semiconductors** (see page 28).

Aluminum is a tough but lightweight metal. It is the most reactive poor metal and is also a good conductor. Its reactivity actually protects it from corrosion. The surface of the aluminum reacts with oxygen very quickly, forming a dull gray layer. This thin layer of corrosion creates a barrier between the air and the rest of the aluminum. Because the air cannot touch the aluminum below the gray layer of rust, it does not corrode. Aluminum is used in construction and in aircrafts. Aluminum foil is used to wrap food.

Tin and lead are used together as solder, an alloy that melts easily. It is used to glue metals together. Lead is also easy to shape and was once used to make water pipes. However, we now know that even small amounts of lead in drinking water can cause illness. Lead is also very dense and heavy. It is used in fishing weights and is the main metal in bullets.

Canning Food

The tin cans used to preserve food are actually made of steel, but they are coated with a thin layer of tin. The tin protects the iron from rusting. Rust might make the can crack. The food would leak out and air could get in. Germs in the air would spoil the food.

Lead is one of the densest metals. It weighs 11 times as much as the same amount of water.

Refining Metals

In nature, metals are found mixed up with other substances in rocks. The process used to turn the rock into pure metal is called **refining**. Refining techniques vary from metal to metal.

Minerals are naturally occurring compounds. Many are formed in volcanoes or deep beneath the surface. Minerals that contain metals are very common and are generally found mixed up with others, forming all kinds of rocks. A rock that contains a lot of a metal—either pure or as part of a mineral—is called an **ore**.

The first stage in refining an ore into a metal is mining. Miners are experts at getting rock out from underground. If the ore is deep down, they dig a tunnel or shaft down to it. If the mineral is at the surface, the miners dig it out leaving a large hole, called an open-cast mine.

The next step is to crush the lumps of ore into a powder. That makes it easier to separate the metal from the waste material it is mixed up with.

People have been using bronze, a mixture of pure copper and tin, for at least 6,000 years.

Flash in the Pan

Gold is always found pure in nature. However, large nuggets of gold are very rare. Most of the world's gold occurs as dust. The dust can be washed out of rocks in fast-flowing water. The water is then panned for the gold. Gold hunters scoop up water and look for the glint of heavy gold dust in the swirling water. It is a slow process but worth it!

Some ores contain pure metals mixed into rocks. This is how gold is normally found in nature, as tiny specks of dust inside rocks. In the past, water was used to wash the gold dust out after the rock had been crushed up. Today, a more powerful chemical called cyanide is used in a process called **leaching**. The gold dust dissolves in the cyanide in the same way salt dissolves in water.

Many ores are formed of metal oxides. These are compounds where the metal has reacted with oxygen. Most iron and copper ores are oxides. The metal is purified by a chemical process that takes place in an extremely hot furnace called a smelter. Smelters have been used for thousands of years and still work in more or less the same way.

The ore is mixed with a fuel containing a lot of carbon. This could be charcoal (a wood fuel) or coal, which is a carbon-rich rock that burns. The fuel burns deep in the smelter, reacting with oxygen in the air.

Purifying metals from their ores requires a lot of heat so the impurities are burned away.

Digging up ore has produced a huge hole in the ground at this mine.

That reaction forms carbon monoxide **gas**. This gas also burns easily and turns into another gas, carbon dioxide. To do this, however, the carbon monoxide needs more oxygen atoms. It takes them from the ore, leaving behind pure metal. The metal melts and trickles out of the bottom of the furnace.

In the case of iron, the metal in the smelter is still full of impurities, such as carbon, sulfur, and silicon. The carbon is blasted out by jets of hot oxygen gas. Calcium is used to clear up the silicon, while magnesium removes the sulfur.

Some metals are so reactive they stay in ore form during **smelting**. A more powerful system is needed to purify them. The metals react to form ores by giving away electrons. **Electrolysis** is a process that uses an electric current to force those electrons back onto the metal atoms. That reverses the reaction and splits the ore into its pure ingredients, including the original metal. This method is much more expensive than smelting. It is used to purify metals like aluminum, magnesium, potassium, and sodium.

Frankenstein's Monster
In the early 1800s, Humphry Davy used electricity to purify several new metals. Mary Shelley heard about this famous work and also how electricity could make dead muscles twitch. She used this idea in her book Frankenstein, *the story of a dead body brought back to life by electricity.*

Precious Metals

Gold, silver, and platinum are said to be precious metals.
They are precious because they are very rare and do not corrode.
These features make them good for use as money and jewelry.

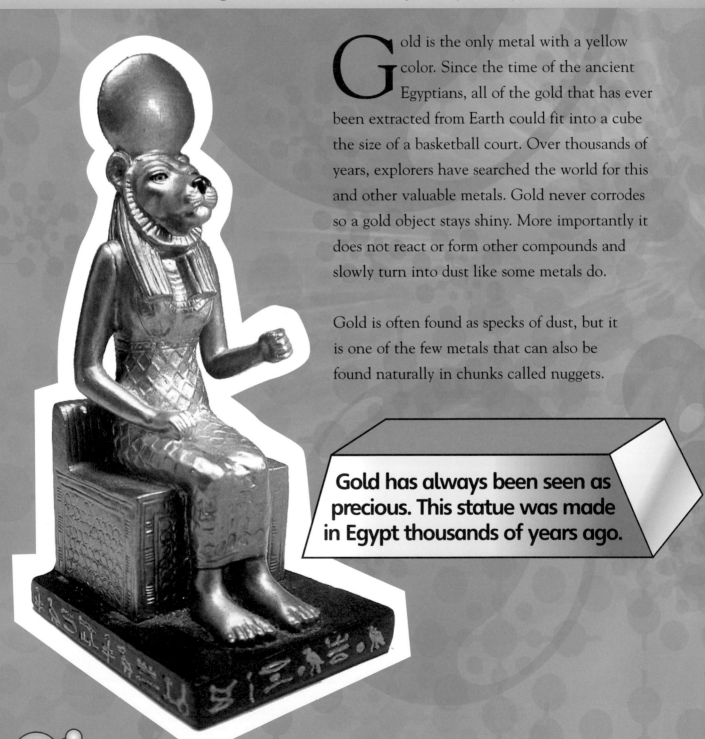

Gold is the only metal with a yellow color. Since the time of the ancient Egyptians, all of the gold that has ever been extracted from Earth could fit into a cube the size of a basketball court. Over thousands of years, explorers have searched the world for this and other valuable metals. Gold never corrodes so a gold object stays shiny. More importantly it does not react or form other compounds and slowly turn into dust like some metals do.

Gold is often found as specks of dust, but it is one of the few metals that can also be found naturally in chunks called nuggets.

Gold has always been seen as precious. This statue was made in Egypt thousands of years ago.

Nuggets are normally quite small, usually not much larger than a pebble. When someone finds a nugget, it can cause a "gold rush" as people dash to the area hoping to get rich. There were big gold rushes in North America and Australia in the 1800s and they occur in places like Brazil and Africa even today.

Fortune seekers from all over the world traveled great distances to get to gold fields before all the metal had been mined. Some became rich, but most did not.

Most gold we see is actually an alloy. Pure gold is so soft that you can scratch it with a fingernail. Gold is often combined with harder and less expensive metal, such as silver or copper, for making jewelry that is tough enough to wear.

Silver is more reactive than gold. It reacts slowly with other chemicals, a process called tarnishing. The tarnish needs to be rubbed off with polish to make the silver shine. Platinum is very unreactive but it is used as a catalyst. A catalyst helps other chemicals react but does not get used up in the process. A platinum catalyst is used in cars to clean pollution from the exhaust.

Space-Age Material

Corrosion on electrical connectors can block the current. Gold never corrodes so it is used in the best electrical plugs. Gold is also used for shields on spacecraft. In space, the radiation coming from the Sun can hurt astronauts and damage machines. However, just a thin sheet of gold foil blocks it out.

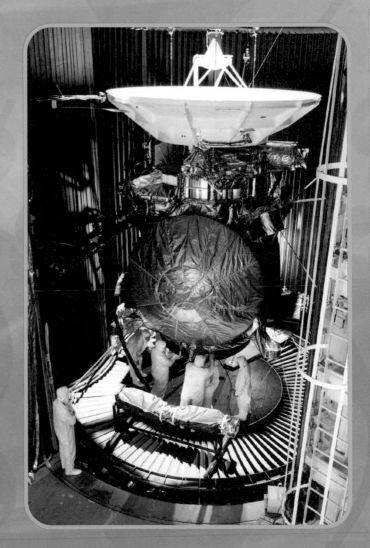

Magnetism

Some metals can be magnetic. They give out a force that pushes and pulls on similar metals. **Magnetism** is linked to electricity, and magnets are used to male electric currents.

Iron, cobalt, and nickel have magnetic properties. Magnetism is the physical characteristic of attracting or repelling (pushing away) metal objects. It was first described in magnetite, a magnetic type of rock found in nature. Lumps of this material are sometimes called lodestones. Planet Earth is also a magnet. The magnetism comes from the spinning iron core.

Today, magnets are made from pure metals. Most are mainly steel but the strongest ones have small amounts of rare metals such as neodymium and samarium. Electromagnets are made from unmagnetic iron which becomes magnetic only when it is electrified. They are useful because they can be turned on and off.

Every magnet has two poles, north and south. The poles are the point on the metal where the magnetism is strongest. If left to hang and move on its own, a magnet's north pole will always point to Earth's north. The south pole will point the other way. When a magnet is broken into pieces, each piece will have a north and south pole.

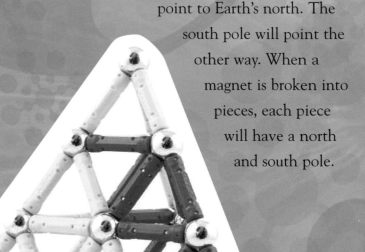

Magnets can attract each other—making this pyramid—but they also repel, or push each other away.

Magnetic Breakfast

Iron is essential for a healthy body; it is an important component of blood. We get iron naturally from many foods. Iron is magnetic, and you can use that fact to find the metal in some foods. Mix a bowl of cereal containing 90% of the daily recommended amount of iron with water. Leave it to form a mush in a clear bag. After a few hours, turn the bag over and put a powerful magnet on it. The iron in the food will collect as a dark spot around the magnet.

When two magnets are placed near each other, their opposite poles will attract one another. When two alike poles come together magnets repel each other. Magnets also attract objects made of iron, cobalt, or nickel, even if they are not magnets themselves. The force from a magnet gets weaker the farther away it is.

Earth is a magnet. The magnetic points of a compass are attracted to Earth's poles.

Metalloids

Not all elements are metals or non-metals; some are half-way in between. Metalloids have properties of both metals and non-metals.

Chemists are not sure how many elements are truly metalloids. They all agree that boron, silicon, germanium, arsenic, antimony, and tellerium belong to this class of element. However, some think polonium is a metal and astatine is a non-metal. Finally, livermorium is so rare **chemists** are just guessing that it might be a metalloid.

Silicon is the most common and important metalloid. Like many of the metalloids, silicon is a semiconductor. A semiconductor can be a conductor and also act as an insulator. Sometimes it carries electricity and sometimes it blocks it. This ability makes it ideal in making the complex but tiny electronic switches in the microchips used in modern technology.

A microchip is made from a single piece of pure silicon, which has a circuit of switches and other electronics cut into its surface.

Realgar is a beautiful mineral that contains arsenic, one of the most common metalloids.

Germanium and arsenic are also used to make semiconductors. So is tellurium, which is an important component in the solar panels that make electricity from sunlight.

Arsenic is one of the most poisonous elements. It is used to preserve wood, preventing bugs and molds from damaging it. Arsenic minerals sometimes mix into drinking water from wells. The poison works slowly. People drinking contaminated water will get headaches and diarrhea before eventually going into a coma and dying.

The main use of boron and antimony, the remaining metalloids, is for fireproofing. Plane-loads of boron compounds are dropped on wild fires.

Hot Mine

Death Valley, California, is known as the hottest place in America. Today it is a tourist attraction, but in the 1880s miners worked there to dig up borax. Borax is a mineral containing boron that is used in cleaners. The Death Valley product was called 20-Mule-Train Borax. That is how many mules were needed to haul the mineral out of the hot valley.

California's hot and dry Death Valley now attracts tourists from around the world.

Glossary

alloy A mixture of metals

atom The smallest unit of an element

charge The property of ions and some subatomic particles; objects with an overall negative charge attract objects with a positive charge. Things with the same charge push each other away.

chemist A scientist who studies the elements and figures out how substances are formed from combinations of atoms

compound A substance made up of two or more elements that have combined during a chemical reaction

conductor A substance that transmits energy as heat and electricity

corrosion When pure metals react with oxygen, water, or another substance in the environment

ductile The characteristic of a substance indicating that it can be stretched and pulled without breaking

electrolysis A process that uses electric current to separate metal from its ore

electron A tiny negatively charged particle that is found in atoms

electron shell One of the layers in which electrons are arranged around the outside of an atom

element A simple natural substance that cannot be simplified into any other ingredients

gas The state of matter where a substance is made up of particles that move independently in all directions

insulators Materials that do not conduct heat or electricity easily

ion A charged particle that is formed when an atom loses or gains one or more electrons

leaching The process of using chemicals to dissolve a metal out of an ore

lustrous When something is shiny

magnetism Having a magnetic field

malleable The characteristic of a substance indicating that it can be bent and hammered without breaking

melting point The temperature when a solid turns into a liquid

metal One of the hard, shiny, opaque elements that conducts energy

metalloid Any of the elements that share properties of metals and non-metals

molecule A combination of atoms that are arranged in a certain way

neutron A subatomic particle with no charge

non-metal An element that is not a metal; non-metal atoms have a lot of electrons in their outer shells

ore Rock that contains a valuable metal

proton A subatomic particle with a positive charge

refining The process of purifying metal out of source rock

semiconductor A substance that can be a conductor or an insulator

smelting The process of extracting metal from ore by burning off the oxygen in an extremely hot oven

Index

Web Finder

www.ptable.com

www.howstuffworks.com/iron.htm

http://gwydir.demon.co.uk/jo/minerals/metals.htm

www.chem4kids.com/files/atom_bonds.html